Elliotté P. Joel

Wounded Poems

ISBN 978-80-570-4759-9

To my beloved friend Susan Myers Nottet

Dear Reader,

Wounded Poems is a damned book, godforbidden
and heavy. I was young. I was so very young and
I knew much more than I do now. Nonetheless,
I reminisce with love on how I was, with pain, falling
in a deep sleep of nothingness.

Having begun my first literary work, which you are
holding right now, dear Reader, at the age of 15,
little did I acknowledge what awaits me. Finishing
the manuscript, aged 19, I was soon to be cured of
my illness solely by writing. All of the three chapters
can speak like a small piece of hell that has
escaped by my hand, thus <u>what I dedicate to all
who suffer is to write. And to hope. Hope will always
live on as long as you love.</u>

Elliotté P. Joel

Žilina, 02/03/2023

Daisy valley

Lightning and rose, try of mine

to a good friend

I stare faintly into crowds, deep down into roach
holes. Herds of cockroaches. They just go and go,
forward without persistent thoughts, awareness of
self. They live through everything. Cockroach can
lose one of its legs, ramble in the unfamiliar. It
doesn't stock its food. Roaches had future, will.
I don't think I have any.

I peer into mirrors, expecting. Endless hoards of
papers are ladies of my time. Hours, months,
witching days. I have morbidly obese feelings – they
can't even walk on their own. They shan't fit into any
thoughts.

You always mention daisies, you must like them
very much. I wonder whether you struggle to cut
your nails because they are really long on your
dominant hand and short on the other one. You
stand nigh mirrors summoning a flow of words.
Words oscillating gently as in rye. Nightly mirrors
and sleepless slumbers. Poems of nonsense and
reveries of being. One day I shall fall into better
darkness of pens and ink. I shall drown in written
words doing what I love, resurrecting as a roach in
a qualmless flight...

Love

Writing regenerates my soul. Cleanses it from all that filth... Conventions, televisions and car drivers who purposely splash walkers on rainy days. Morning airness nourishing coal soots lowering from heavens. Streets we are unfree to walk coated in blind unbright milk. On a log of departed willow sits a sleepy water nymph and out of boredom she tickles all tulips into venomous delirium. Yet, I no longer slave to uncertain anxieties. I shall no more slouch naked on a bench in center, asking strangers: "Are you my father? Are you my brother or friend?"

What I knew has been draining me and what I didn't has made me lost. Old quills seem distant and strange. New quills seem like black veins, lines which cross each other until they eat out entire page with their hollowness.

It's impossible to be taught anything. You can be told where to find it, you can be shown or awed by another human being, yet it's you who must learn it yourself, alone. And the older we grow the less we ask questions.

They have hidden thirsty moon and dismembered it into silver stones. Skeleton that was left we call Thirsty moon: exorbitant restaurants, unconditional sacrifices of happiness.

"Is it love?"

Voyage of understanding spread to ashes has glued
with realization that it is, indeed, love. Then the
name which is carrying today's date was buried
forgotten.

Meadow lullaby: The land of silence

Sparkle seen but so shortly glows very little. My dried flowers and tiny beauties of rain-stained windows entertain no longer than few eternal days. Their lovely letters flee with the first summer storm.

I never rest on anybody's shoulder. I fit into everybody's arms but only when I don't try to. Yellow words fall into unpeeled layers, tenderly sounding through caves to be smothered in the farthest mazes.

My soul does not levitate between petals to the sky of belonging. It's not a light that would flash your noon reveries. It's a feeble reflection of my blunted self.

Land of silence shall saunter in the calmest dreams. Liquid sun, wider company of meadows, no claws of reality, naught spoken in vile human whispers. Heed a radiant play of herbs and wind, garden queens, wildflowers, excluding man-made time. Pencil-drawn pastel clouds chant to your muses and make them dance in your head. Linear skyfires release a perfume of novel subconsciousness that knows no sorrow. It is aware briefly of sparkles seen every night which lighten roads of lost maddened souls.

New poem

Before my sleep is retrieved I visualize all my terrible chess moves. If a chessboard could weep it would... It would propel away its pieces and begin to fly with noisy clapping of wood against wood, and jump into hearth.

Who could have guessed? Since I no longer possess the board I can tell you about glimmering fields that screamed with dew every morning. I would lie on ground and solve crosswords. I can do it very fast. It's the only thing I'm good at. I can't talk nor paint nor flow with any kind of norms. I would solve crosswords while waiting for Sam. After Sam would arrive he would sit next to me and solve his own crosswords. Grass and its flowers above were blunted by our silence. Our silence reveried about affection of flowers towards its grass below.

Now my hand feels not mine. It slips away to worse and worse muses, worse romances that have died over five years ago. My eyes are thirsty for arson which dissolves conventions. Every novel flame ends up adored, muscular, accompanied by sociable women who live off their spark, while I fashion by distance with left out chess pieces...

Reaching of eternal life

Violets. Violets have been frozen even before they could bloom.

In this eternity I found that conscience of mine is old. It dampers and clears my young body.

What was it that made my soul so ancient and miserable, pure with blitheness of colorful streets, grass below?

Were it unaware children lunging through blocks of flats whom I couldn't play with for my grave realization that present innocence shall be forgotten soon?

Was it my family, tossing away obsolete gramophone, fancied before on countless dances, to garbage while I was at school?

Was it melancholic rain waltz of August that only my ears could hear? Was it torment of this strange mankind? Were it cigarettes I have stolen or borrowed without returning?

In case it matters, since then I am seeing violets.

Violets. Forever preserved meanwhile still growing. And at the same time - dead.

Ashes

If only I was a stone in a brook sheltering
microscopic water creatures... If only I was the
sun... If only I didn't die.

I don't want to think about jewish badges and his
harrowing experiments. They still cannot breathe,
their own walls are digesting them. How many times
they wished to be there, away from cruelties of
outer world...

Then my ashes fleed to sky and fate put them on
top of yours. You have left daisies for your mother
so that she doesn't cry and now you plant them for
everyone who can still see beauty of life. Was it you
to send me buzzing of bees? Smell of rain? Wind
made by melodies?

Not even his needles shall part our joys.

Prescribtion of bleak rooms

A lone boat that consumes you like a fly would
consume a bit of sugar? Children staring, shouting,
contemplating, lying? I have never felt like a child.
More as if I was something heavily light and
intangible, barely real, on a border. I don't even like
to chat about politics. It reminds me of hell.

Rooms were cement and lone boats back on pills
now reel off a lot about responsibility when they
actually mean obedience. Before morrow, have one
plea, an overwhelming urge to walk around the
house and hear its silence. Complexity present in
the mundane allows us to escape and transfer
learned knowledge to mereness it really is.

Nazi ballet of waterlily monsters fascinates by
normality... Condemn it! Forget it! If you don't know
what to do set your writings on fire, toss them out on
the street and think about dirty stuff. In a war with
my fragility, why do I have to feel so much?

There, where beer dancer shall bring a sour
summer, you step on the acme of your pierceful
walk, on the acme of silver sand. Saunter forest
lines along the peak and unripe sun is a savior,
wind, earth and its tall grass embrace you as if it
was love returned after many deaf years.

My foal days, which have been lacerated and shot
before my eyes, found a stripe from a dream.
Pierced by bullets like an old can, yearning fulfilled:
I am enfolding it, drinking it down. Thus I prescribe

you insanity in a rainstained season, away from
needles, lobotomy, those are grains of sand where
trunks and saffrons reign. During a circular walk,
miles-long, you will discover that in some houses
there are no locks. The illness. It was an orange
sleep in which we did not live.

Gymnastics

Solitude of corals, dying pulse of animate sand overcame an ancient era. Sheer grief trudged along with snow. But snowflakes were yet too big, yet too round, they took pain and carried numbness.

Gymnasts spread their legs to jump high. When I deem about it, there is nothing that makes a gymnast special. All used to be left out of plays and cannot spell, just like me.

I revisited lakes I had made and I did not recognize them for they should flow with beauty. My petite ponds of filth befuddled me that I have seen their dignity. I had been attempting to harness branches to mark stable points of my conscious mind only to burn them down.

Nevertheless, destruction breeds creation. Then gymnasts can jump even higher.

Don't try

I can hear cries of trees. They cry because they are
lonely. I sleep inside pink clouds that smell like time
swallowed by dusk. After lying down yellow stars
above roll on like obsolete films in company of blue
butterflies that bring forgetting. I can only think of
burning tables and foreign hands.

Once I had a pride to build myself a pleasant castle
shimmering with sun's thread and pearly velvet of
snow. My yelping head lacked eyes to see and ears
to hear that, in fact, it was no great home.

Tomorrow I'll become an eerie shadow, a stain on a
suit. At least I wish I was made out of breeze so
I don't grieve when I stomp even on a single flower.

Delusions of an unknown fever

Queen Winter befell the land and drifted me into insanity by riddled wind. Its snowstorm was sewed by the last remnants of stars, yet with long lost wonders of what is it to sleep or to be awake.

Winter kissed me with a tender acid on its lips. The coldest season's warmth bestowed me uncertain imaginary mysteries. I shy to reveal more but that I've seen love in my dreams and believed it.

Nobody wants to dance

The center grooves with winter markets, street shopping cocaine lines. Perceptions which whisper to me what to write have stepped in disgrace on every maiden. Some colorful ornaments met yearned deaf shape by their own sorrowful loneliness.

Love is a needle too sharp. Vampire chokes on its sore throat. He unbuttoned my pelerine and caught pissed off clouds condensing into frozen moon nightwater.

"Why don't you dance?"

Dry tears ball my cheeks in a dancewhile daze. Alone I weep.

Liquor stores

I.

Who would comprehend people, their tiny
hopelessness of bending over for oddly round
shards of whisky bottles, uncountable midnight
agony of drying one's own tears with a nearby-lying
sock? Kind heart's pain of those who collect
cigarette butts at bus stops, who are heading to
liquor stores with comforting tortures of first loves:
Mayas and Veronicas, Patricks and Roberts?
Recollections of July nights are as bright as angels,
yet still they crush what they see, from distance of
a dark corner. But a little missing whiles it takes for
us to crumble, for dead strings to thicken.

II.

I wished to never meet him again, long before
tender symphony of seashells sensed like a soul
hundred years old. Azure of Ocean soon caressed
me elsewhere, to soft radiant waves on its top.

He would deepen my wounds, he would make me
feel dirty. In Ocean I would face my mind's yearning
– depth of subconscious connection, where I find
simple words reading:

I love you, deeply. With my head. With my heart.

His strings of me are dense. He used to say we
were made for each other. He is on his way to buy
some booze. You are my Ocean but what do I know

about cliffs? Might I grow a fishtail or might I cease
by your freezing surface...

What raindrops do not understand

to you

I.

Raindrops on blooming herbs in Saturday idle
outside vile windows on the first floor grapple to
realize shortness of their existence. That there will
be less and less of their bodies as minutes knock
from below wooden boards of bed. Raindrops don't
even know they're raindrops. And so they don't that
upon fake plastic stars I used to reverie about
something greater than frightened mute fences to
overcome my loneliness which is some sort of
nauseous tinfoil that fashions me detached, far.
I used to reverie about somebody who could speak
languages of breeze and sky murals of kites.

II.

No time of day abounds with light more than night.
When one walks past midnight whole clarity of
previous crimes malforms to belong to another –
old, twisted, already buried. Yet this piece isn't
about imaginary funerals of our past selves.

I shouldn't be trying to calm those underfed crows
feasting on day's attention: whether my
reminiscence drives through your head, whether it
drive with a flat tire. I shouldn't be trying whatever at
all.

You stand by kitchen counter. Your heart cheers up when you talk about something swell. You light my cigar. Your umbrella doesn't allow but a tear of heaven's cry to get to me.

But the raindrops don't know. I should tell them as soon as I arrive home although they won't be there anymore. Raindrops don't know I am happy.

White hearts, my heart seems to dance on piano keys

What am I missing? I'm young, blond, and my heart is shriveled like an ugly wound. It was stupider than winking angels on poker cards, I always turned across another street to find myself another true love though I am true love of nobody.

... without borders and names, and forced dread of needs, without conventions... Through a slot where curtain ghost hesitates between doors I glanced at my heart dancing on the floor whilst you played, then it danced on piano keys and then it set itself on breeze, feeling no cold, unbonded by distance or physical touch.

In all lucidity of shapes and colors, I quivered in the playground of imagination. Teethy heavy sunrays were shattering on windows as if they could absorb dullness of glass, they have just chosen not to. Although sun's petals had been silenced by artificial transparent alien they did project on the other side, clambered as their mother Sun moved on her voyage. Without a barcode tattooed on bride's neck... Without ether-colored lambent purple, my heart seems to dance on sun.

It's not a thing you'd hear from people: love as certain as by moonshine and clammy window dew.

Parades of cool June moon, crowd hearts and saddening morning blueness are over.

Early poems selection (2017 – 2019)

See the shattering smoke

Scarcely I find the will to taste present, to enjoy
a meal. Everything turned blind. They killed my
beloved past, youth has faded after the blast. See
the shattering smoke, how it rises and falls down.

I had but one life. Joy has been disturbed, frivolities
murdered so I soak in sadness: runny times have
stood, runny days went further. Disappearing in the
smoke - will to live, love and boldness - see the
shattering smoke. The most special change, the
best dies soaking strange, soaking in lies - the
curse of being immortal and neverchanging.

In my purse I hold my innocence, my pureness and
it drowns, it drowns in an empty place. It never had
any face. My worthless innocence long gone
presents that it's beauty subtly drawn but I see it as
sorrow of my lost will.

Loss

In a windy place, cold shiver ran along his spine.
Lighting the first cigarette. No good from his eye, no
kindness of face. She was not glad. Fear, shame,
distorted sense of self. The desire for catastrophe
was not real.

The loss of will has been achieved, knowing what
happens, fully aware of disgusting drill not as painful
as believed. No hell neither cross, farewell, delusion
of cleaningness.

Desks and pipe finches

Every day I see her in doorway. She keeps
scrubbing, picking, fidgeting like any way upright
unimaginable. Every daylight. Desirable insanity,
pierce right through audience. Back covered while
slice open. Hidden skin under reckless vice of her
hands that write, hands that point, that can't stop.
Unstable churl. Nothing but a pile of rage... That's
how I destroyed multiple pieces of furniture for my
thoughts.

Beware bathroom, all mirrors. You can hear birds in
pipeholes. Pick them all out. They taste bitter, look
bloated, bare and boneless... The finch dies in dirt
by the very first touch. Your clothes, your walls
stained with corpses of birds. But it calls, you need
to do it.

You are going to forget

Ouch   Ouch

The Heart   Is Getting

Dry The Heart On The

Floor Cracking At The

Bottom At Night

In Daylight

Ouch

The sight on pedestrian bridge

The summer of drawing sounds signed by whistling on hazel acorns, ponderous ambles with full pockets, was jinxed. A poor man on a bridge trembled in a hole-eaten cloth, leg and arm were missing, fingers falling soft to soon never be felt. The unknown beggar was inappropriate for expectations of wide bridge: street painters, traders, fishermen and mimes.

I began to fear of trees' leaves, that it will fall in weeks to river. Of the fear I did not cross the bridge, then there was fall and winter...

Soldiers of steel, whistling into dark, by them I returned. I leaned over a fence. Water was being brushed by sun. Once again: street painters, traders, fishermen and mimes.

Barefoot days, I wish I would have never turned eighteen

When children play by brooks during desertlike days, busy building boats, aiming to behand lightly flowing fish, they stamp over rocks for the homely, mellow earth.

Sun of fire is sitting on a shore. Vail of heavy sand sticks dust, beads, dirt... Yet this does not crust momentous as the earth warms, of that it loves and cherishes its little souls.

I am wording my onely wish of child coffins for which I am too tall. My boots are peeking out. Summer rite evens ensnare. Bed will swallow the child and digest. Heartless arm dislimbs the flies' wings. Now, the fork of flies is used for wine of fingers. Why does time come so bitter to me?

To be heading to eternal holiday, into missed age which have been unnoticed, timid, effortless and in that was its raindrop kiss, heartfelt fresh promenades, caressing hands - begone! Begone, standing between doors!

The meadow never sleeps, justly oscillating in gale. I cycled up to dandelion wild to be preached by woods in the village of unheard name. And I rode down, down the hill, trail strengthened by tappering swift pathway, topless.

I have dreamt that I was a soccer player who distanced himself in a sneak to lie on soccer field

fake grass. Deceiving artificial texture, deceiving
tribunes, deceiving game and players. On ground in
idle freedom. Doors up to sky, clouds moved
brightly and very fast.

Boys on the hill

Open the window, brother. It is winter, it is holiday time. Sledging down to withering plane tree, boys on hill drag their tiny joys and sledges. Do not strike your friend. Do not strike the withering plane tree. Do not thwart snowing until May.

Until we cease cherishing will to breathe, until we fall in grief, we are the boys on the hill, yet, we laugh. Until lamps begin to shine we stay out on the hill and until we die we will play nigh brook.

Stars' tale of bohemian spring

Grey-brown suits dulling through grey-brown streets and grey-brown blocks... Sleep under a suburban sky could enthrall that there is more behind that haze – voyageful ponder. To starve of a lack of known and to glut on a surplus of dazeful perseverance. During night, always, of a pointless wander I dream.

Touch, poetry of extracted teeth

Every opening of eyes is like inhalation after rise
from chlorine pool: from water to air through that
nameless line, airwater. Solitary I pressed rhymes
on marble of paper. In evening, I saw that I possess
forty-five on skin. Face hurt up from nurses and
cheekbones.

Senses have blunted me even without chemical
substances. I fell to my knees, they buried a finger
into my head and I puked heavy rhymes on their
wandersome boots. Heavy rhymes are purgatory.
Light ones are moorbirds.

Poet´s kisses for syllables and, too, to meadows,
forests, seasons, love, innovation. From height of
thirteen feet, holding hands, we capered into a dried
river and became untamed.

The pile of rage and sorrow

Holy virgin

Miles were tattered in her muddy shoes. She was yet again like a muddled oak leaf. Where to fly and where to land, she did not know for herself. She said: "I am worried that I am not young anymore. All of us have played on an unkept paddock gaunt by sun and dirt, with ruby smiles, palms sculpted out of satin, fed by oversugared cakes, until the lanky figure of life approached and signated us on foreheads with its burnt soiled claw."

Soul of stones that went on a foremorning walk saw the foxtrot of melancholy, and after her lone dance was over she lied on the ground, dead like a dried up earthworm on a pavement. The soul remarked: "Those glorifying immortality and beauty, and eternal innocence shall never find it. Moths that circle in a moony reflection of transparent eye neglect the waving of truculent grass, along with their tragedy, their unspeakable sorrowness. The key is to deem, day by day. For the everlasting youth must you be never young, for the neverending childhood must you never be a child. Then you are sentenced to eternity, be not afraid of the cease of your heart, it shall not door you. And if it has already, the memory of his terrible, beautiful footsteps had vanished by a swing of the backdoor of your recollection... throughout dried up rye, nigh urban blocks of flats, brooks, alleys,..."

Girls who climb the highest trees

Squinting, I cannot see the midnight rain. Night's velvet mirror twists like clay on pottery wheel, human illusions get to be too outermost and vanish as mirrors may no longer reflect. You must stand nigh, feed your eyes and fingers, there are so many.

Wilderness calls, persisting your drive to commit death of your changeable self. I shall be different from now on. Unbonded by statement of my established personality caged by people I know and what they perceive me as. I would sculpt a new person out of the previous which has been destructed and thrown shapeless the moment I've decided to leave. Everyone gives a piece of their heart to rude girls, those who sneeze quietly like mice, climb trees and don't cry for pinned butterflies. Nearing summer. Haze. Their ardor for people doesn't shrivel like an unwatered rose.

A child returning as a figure of the evening by the strike of street lamps would never come home if they could decide because who would? It's terror on fragile left out souls afraid of loud sounds, who fidget too much and don't understand anything. It's too late to have a father but I can still put on that pearly fake Vegas smile.

"Does youth exist only to be sacrificed?" asked H. Miller or who. I am not sure when exactly do souls grow up. Why do rose petals fall before their flourishing if they've been crushed unbloomed?

After the vanishing of an owner, her foam raspberry-colored dress remains covered in moths, only to age into a couple of hanging strings and spiderwebs. And it doesn't have a dad. And it doesn't have a lover. And it even has nobody. But at least it's obedient.

Of two sisters and Soap

Soap idles next to a mirror. Not a sunray relishes on it. Soap is pale, it's getting skinny. Washed and shaved, I become a feast for nobody that will again get spoilt and oily after two days.

I like my hair so greasy it looks like strings of meat slouched over hooks. I like my ribcage pain and dirt on my neck, nails as long as a witch, bent back, puss in my cracked feet, breath putrid. I like it somehow. I feel as if it is bringing me closer to death.

Sixteen, seventeen, eighteen, nineteen. Nineteen bugs on the ceiling want not to disturb me, scrambled mistakes mean no harm, irregular black circles mark the white creek of my disordered thinking. I wonder about touch. I've been held in embrace by fewer people than I've been to bed with. The other night there came over a hundred bugs for visitation, they went after light. I crouched on the sheets and I felt like the queen of insects. It was not a true tragedy. I know two sisters on the edge of town who cannot do anything. The older, Susan, has nothing, no beauty nor smarts and she is just eating the food I buy her for handful of kisses after the younger sister took you away.

People are not at peace with innocence because they don't know what it is. They define it as devouring certain actions while it's indeed but keeping the soul you were given in spite of how

much wrong was committed on it. Our jollies were
evening windows buried under a frozen white duvet,
determined cold has overtaken it thereby
snowflakes twinkled like light feathered soots. The
winds and reticent snow were laming to its
motherland. People like to go in lines. People like to
walk on roads they can see.

Soap. You made me cleaner than clean.

Fool, the nun of brief visitation

And yet again, one by one, I am burning pages of my books. Every meal tastes like polyester, it crinkles in between my teeth like a roadkill whoever can stab with a stick until there is dead restless snow in those fleshy hollows where should be the heart. Over and over again, I am discarding drafts and concepts about kitschy dreams.

I could not even sleep, her poisoned haze suffocated me as if a frigid enormous vise throttled my throttle. Her hair possesses fragrance of heaven. Her eyes are open and never blink. She is within all walls.

Infernal grief bleeds all over your hands which hold her… Bronze vows told you of deceiving thus I am thrown yet again into pits of hell. One more time, poems about you and me burn.

The arrival of a priest

How much time do you have? Lots of time? Would you like to have a beer? Would you like some butter on your bread? Indeed, nobody truly enjoys poems about love. The majority of eyes feed on despair. They crowd behind a glass door to watch unrightfulness jerking off above someone or something fragile.

It's raining in the bedroom again. You must have left a window open for angels to come. And we got a thick little cloud instead. I always feel so safe just with you but outside you are so cold, distant like asphalt glory towered upon deserted fountain in a loom.

Longing in flames which render my revealed body full of sobbing illusory cracks coated in latex bark, it's diagnosis is psychosis – a beheaded rose which has been lost nameless. You encounter all. You see all. You sense all. You endure cries of all, fates of all, but they will never tell you why. Daisies whisper about lust as their dirt drips down on my head. I feel so scoffed by them.

The worst thing is that I know I'm not going to die anytime soon, decades and decades are approaching and licking their lips when they linger about how they're going to crush me. I have become a farce of myself and my view is empty, yawning into the farthest lands, belonging only and only to the field, the clock is almost ripe, I should

harvest it or I will be out of time by winter, told me
the approaching priest. Thus I stand and chant
about your eyes that bling like transparent sea
mirroring every sunray to all moles so they can eat
the crops faster.

Burial

How does a jeweler mend a broken goose feather?
By love wounds. And cherry tobacco.

A big grey cloud above a valley sensed a tickle on
its warts-covered spine made out of frivolous dark
circles of dance. It was sun's summerly daze.
Ravens are here, not above the country and not
hidden by murks.

I know some homeless people drink cleaning
equipment, they filter it with a piece of bread so they
don't get blind while they pour it in their eyes.
Bleeding maples, crinkled floor, gone rhythm, snail
sand and noise, I know you have changed me
forever. I flow through days like a ghost in restless
pace, to school and then ponder with blisters
because if I come home it'll hit me.

Blue roses shall replace my lies for they are glum,
they are born and withering from the pasture of their
soil: goodbye, sweet slumber, farewell, I will write
and heal from the mud of ocean sheep! No more
lithium love, no more sobs for desert's death! It was
a long time to lose between currents of misery,
infinite grenades deranged to the extent of my
youth. Shadows were avoiding me. I've been
swimming away from a shore in hope to die of
exhaustion and I've been riding my bike against

highway, soring living parts that were to be pampered, my heart, my soul and mind.

You keep looking for it, that tobacco that would veil your essence, for the darkest of a kind to overpower expressionless hallways, for the strongest of a kind to overcoat heels battling asphalt with smiles as they move.

It's not your fault nor Simone's. It's my sins. It has always been needed for me to abuse myself in a spasm to the transition of hell, heaven, so I could come out of the earth of my expectations. Nightless seventeen, farewell, Paris, Madrid, Berlin, London, Moscow and Rome! Outcasted to the end of universe. The prose is heavy and dreary, what do I even know about life? – Everyone is forgiven and florets that shall grow on my grave are me.

New emotional famine, raw

Pine forests in the middle of a desert, artificial like
two lovers kissing through a plastic bag, I like such
ugliness. Perhaps it's on purpose, perhaps it's
a revolt, perhaps doctors know. Although I doubt
I could be helped. At home I even have
a tremendous machine for stories, lurid and eldrich,
I named it Memory.

Sometime close to midnight it spits out a few papers
full of numbers and codes, for instance:

"Hi."

"Hello, how are you?"

"Fine, how about you?"

"Good."

"How old are you?"

"Seventeen, you?"

"Fourteen. Do I look bad?"

"No, I've seen uglier. Do you want to do it?"

"I don't know."

"Where will we walk?"

"I don't know."

"I don't know either."

Tender bones, purplish veins tangling its ways. His hand itself felt lifeless, numb, like holding a wax figure deprived of limbs or holding a Saturday piece of raw meat.

"Which school do you go to?"

"None, I dropped out."

"I would, too, if I could. I don't like people."

"Why? Did they hurt you?"

"Probably not. I don't know."

I distrust that I have ever been human. You step on little plants because they're in your way and when they flourish they still have a scar. Colorful, in full bloom, permanently wretched. Look over them, you don't want them in your bouquet. You just hate them because they're ugly. I sit on a front porch and visualize collecting them so that they can burn.

"Nevermind. Just give me a little kiss and everything will be okay again."

I wish I could see behind the sky but it never ends.

Ashtray beach and Rochester's insane wife

Whenever I saw an article about a tragic death of someone young, whenever I saw madmen, painters and actors, queers, gangsters, wankers, women standing along the roads, elders with dementia, the lonesome and dying, trapped, it was a drizzle predicting my core. I used to take a lot of Brontës from library during those times. Jane Eyre and her pitiful suffering... I only liked her when she suffered, otherwise she was quite tedious.

People are either born to be loved and idle or to be artists but I ceased to believe it when the thaw of awful bloodless musk carried me to your waves of ashtray beach. Polaroid holidays without calendar flew below blossoms, when a new wind, the hope of witching season, was born ailing. What is the reason for bitterness, that bloody drink thundering the obsolete must sustain?

Oh, my ears feel it... rambling when you are coming down the stairs. Your presence scares off every sudden silhouette... All chairs at home are broken. The stuff I have brought here is broken. The walls are broken, the floor, the air is dirty and sheets are like rose petals.

I seem to be rebuked over and over by life: Don your smile and raise your drink, now you do know why do roosters sing. As if loving you was the greatest sin. We shouldn't feel a duty to whip ourselves for trying our best when our best is still not enough. Perhaps people are either born to die or to live through everything life bestows them and pay exorbitant prices for it, who knows. You have paid your leasing for thousand deaths, you got your Lolita.

Dying. Dying in tranquility of your newfound merriness as dogs bark, children play and rivers flow. Everything is as it should be.

Losers like you, Flo, have always the best lives in case they live up to adulthood

There is a void behind a verge. I jumped off the verge. The walk was not long. I imagined I have always been walking this way. Not knowing where you go, you pace for days turning into years with vague feeling on a seemingly abandoned path narrowly alone. Alone with all the thoughts and memories which do not feel real.

Uncanny associations approached before slumber. Slash tires, do downers. I have wanted to chop my head off with scissors on every photography of those emerald widows and artificiality of near places behind them. I have confessed my love to him at the age of twelve, he's replied to a friend: "You can have her, I don't want her!" Then he's mixed all colors of plasticine into a brown dough and threw it on the ceiling. It stayed there for two weeks, believe it or not.

You laugh, everyone utters you're insane. You cry, nobody says a word. Even if it makes you happy they want to take it away because you're taught to be a silent, chained thing. Foolish stupidity of escapes and fantasy. Oh, whispers! Inadequate! I locked myself in the bathroom and bawled about my misfortunate decadency. All dreams I have had were around my street. I have radicalized my youth with avantgarde aspirations and dreadful window sombers. I have wallowed in a self-constructed world, my childhood has been a hollow pasture smacked on a glass overcoated by dust.

My seeking of dreams without plans mounted to leave as it saw the nothing dance, ascending higher away from renouncing earth. It was already dark outside and I got cold. I marched home, slightly calmed by a milky duvet snuggling my sireland like a grandfatherly sea vessel. I greeted my mother. We never spoke of that incident again.

It was funny to see death turn on its toe.

Fourteen or fifteen

to Simone

If I was a real writer I'd write about how water
element drooled over to rule with heaviness, to
bring life, to bring death. I drank it as if in thirst,
water was coming out of my nose and mouth as
a spotless vomit, and I drank it again. There were
no pills nor guns.

I had short hair and one loose pants like a boy.
I wore them even in June, close to passing out of
heat. Not a body would crawl near me as if I was
a smelly tramp. I listened to unpleasant things.
*I almost got a stroke when I saw you! I wouldn't
even use you as a bike holder!* I had my first at
fourteen. I would lent him money for pervitine
because he treated me like a human being and to
this day I have never been with somebody my age.
Fourteen or fifteen, no hugs of an angel, no
endearment.

What for the limbs is first love? Poems and songs,
tales, keep hiving about how it's ought to look,
sound, feel, taste, smell, be. However, nowhere is
stated what should I comprehend it as – the first
symptoms of affection towards another kind?, the
first person whom you screw with?, the first both-
sided transcendation between young minds?

Some people are simply helpless, fearing they'll
perish alone, dreaming about running away into the

woods and eating blueberries, perhaps treeroots
like old witches in medieval age, or taking the
earliest bus to the capital city and finding the
nearest skyscraper. "These are the brightest years
of your life. Enjoy them, Florence. You do not even
understand, yet, how beautiful life is, how beautiful
youth is." awed elders and teachers, words
unspoken smithed me still. But that's no novelty,
everybody writes such poems. If I was a real writer
I'd write about a boy I've seen five or six times, his
mother worked on a conveyor belt, he slept with
a wine bottle next to his bed and alone, he carved
a heart on his arm when he had time and then he
rested his head in his palms and cried.

Charles Bukowski told me about bee's death

to L.

I. School

... I told him back that by being myself I have dug my own grave. And I would do it again.

There is not much to tell. My hair has never been pulled, my shoes have never been stolen. I'd borrow them pencils and they would wipe their hands onto each other's clothes. One day one of them said my mother should had shot herself whilst expecting me because they would. Another time another one of them said that someone would fuck me only if I had a bag over my face. That's more or less all. I said there is not much to tell.

II. Men who love and who want to own, and
don't realize anything

When we met, you and I knew it's cold in hell. So we knew that worst days in summer are best days in winter, our eyes were exactly the same color, they reminded me of dull horses, the golden age of circus.

You were always bringing me apples from home, from uni, or simply from your hands, and they were hard to swallow. "They must be metal," I said. You grabbed one and took a bite, with full mouth you replied: "I just have to get rid of them." Then you almost took your own life. Nothing was like before

57

since. Not that it has ever been love. When we held
hands it was like lying down on winter ground and
waiting for soil to slowly reclaim us.

III. Mourns for the bee

Great writers would deem about a thick foam that
burns to the slightest touch and absorbs me into
awaited limbo while I choke on sand as slimy as
snails. Their feeble echo that wanders without aim
only to settle – on empty display shelves, inside
a porcelain kettle, and hairspray fume – and vanish,
still yelps in whispers. But it's quite different, like
thinking about spilled milk on dinner-cloth or wide
stairs turning into sledding hills in my nightmares.

God knows where I am now. Some days are better,
some worse, my hair smells like cigars and each
night I sleep with centipedes crawling beneath my
heart. Perhaps I had some type of strange bond to
those children, to you.

Everyone has been through greater misfortunes
than one another but one bee dies a billion deaths
because all bees are the same.

We all know I'm dying

They offer here so many and everyone loves to see
me walk my leather boots. The meat at the display
shelf bleeds, from circuses to bars to pageants to
meat, it's always been alluring for mankind to
experience something dead that used to be alive.
I just feel a need to drift away from myself for the
reason it was me who you could not love.

I remember the queer day when we shared a cigar
on your balcony. "It's truly a pity that we don't feel
affection towards one another," you said and went
inside. I stood there like a lobster in boiling water.
"Do you want to finish it?" you asked, handing me
the cigar. "Yeah, sure." I replied

... Tonight I stopped a young man in a lorry. He
promised to drive me home. He was an albino with
something uncanny in his eyes. He told me: "You
see, I like Hendrix and polar bears, and women who
have some meat on their bones."

"Well, I do have a plump friend. Her father is
a butcher although she doesn't hitchhike."

"And how about you, what do you care for? What do
you like?"

"I like to drink."

"What else?"

"Seek."

"Would you like a ham sandwich? I didn't have time to eat it at work."

"No, there is enough death among us."

"Don't say such things. Walking girls never die."

"But there are so many and none of them will ever dream again."

He played a Hendrix cassette and drove me home.

Clean substance

I lied in my bed, alone. I cooked my dinner and sat down, ate it, alone. I gazed at vague boxes and speaking woods. I have distorted the perception of time.

The simpler something is the more difficult it becomes for human mind to comprehend. Delirium of the first endearment? I cannot fall for uncertain certainty that there is no light crunching behind the corner. Who wants, has a shit, I am dying for too long. The chains of rain in longing decried azure tediously owning a single color like desolate age when everyone jumped from one lean branch to another, dreaming of death in a cashmere duvet. Our souls see dimly, realize dimly, it's like drinking coffee with closed eyes. Clean substances are foreign to our egos.

As soon as an abstract term gains a material form we habit to worship it. Why digest spikes? Why would we have to suffer for love? How there can be freedom in restrictions? Self-funerals of our minds? Nauseating pain, inequality? What is the surface for if the skeleton is wrong to the bone? I have become deaf to comprehension.

All poems go in a loop about the same stuff. I write because it's worth to be written. But then those missing pieces on my chest and shoulders, and back, seem to be only good for something pleasing yet meaningless. Like origami. Origami out of paper.

Towering snow is melting on command of birds'
spring opera.

I wonder if I have ever been beautiful.

The arms of my own

The preachers uttered: "Marvin is dying". The
heaven rained with the black revulsion of
a responsible finger, strangeness relished on us. As
if we were staring at an empty beer can. I reckon
she might have been released.

Marvin, with your sweaters and the heavy bed of
angel at mere fifteen, may I stop by, let's say,
today? You can open the sky like the wind while
I imagine your hair is hay to burn witches on. As
walls cry themselves to sleep fog in my head
disquiets me for you have been born to be
cherished by nature or fate unlike me. How small
am I? Small like a single paper you invert so there
can be written something else but still it stays the
same paper? Only arms I've ever been to are arms
of Marilyn.

My mind is a crude place I lumber to fathom.
I question whether I shall ever return.

Wrong egg

At an ungodly hour, as I wrote, I was greeted by a moth with silver wings like pearls in ash thriving to play. Or rather thriving for light or perhaps the best thriving to escape this narrow lore. We all look forward to past too soon.

To someone we have never met and feelings that do not exist.

My uncle has this yacht in the capital city and a few enterprises. My festive glances of imagination have seen that petite English-style mansion through an 8 feet wall.

Summer was visibly losing its power which was being passed to fall, a season filled with playgrounds... and ashes. The colors were venomous, naturally synthetic. The bill from cousin's hotel's café taled about my wish to have a friend, it overwrote that one latte with a pinch of mist, expectations. The days of titans, a chase after light. All that for a wrong egg. I waited by the telephone and he never called and nor did you, brother.

Negative inversion

Every not so high balcony. Every screaming bus driver. Every school barbery. I adore Gemini rising, the longer something is lost the more lost it becomes. The lacking presence is enshadowed by the flow of time and eventually withers as impassive and distant. Every growling winter that blackens the air, Christiane, I remember you.

Walking next to each other without aim, we went far, far to the end of this plain world. Glass eye of your mother was always looking through my soul. You would say: "My mom is a little fucked up."; I asked: "Why?"; you replied: "I don't know. Moms are like that."; I replied: "Are you afraid of death?"; "Very. I can't imagine dying."; "Me too. I don't want to die. I am locked in my cage, eating and sleeping, and shitting, I have never done anything. I wish I was free but I don't know what else would I do.". Cigarettes, heads to sky, you were nude and dry, raw, mundane. It was bearable but sometimes not, sometimes you were choking me.

Many people struggle with knowledge of how avalanches are created. They collect and absorb until they collapse. It's the freedom of tragedy, red like hell, cool to touch. Can one truly be released without torment? Seldom I wish. But it's quite a strange feeling when someone leaves your life. Like they weren't real at all.

Margin

We shouldn't condemn what comes from childhood because it was thought on the peak of our cleanest awareness. Recall that gorgeous edge near grass, greeting you, unwinding a gate to hearth of another world with hurried pollen on a way. The pollen relished on your thin shoes like a film of strenght to listen to those cryptic stories about those whose all senses have been taken and blood spilled for that majestic touch.

The thing which has been tormenting me, yet not so mercilessly to abandon me into remnants of a dusty wreath, was the ardor which murmured and tickled my conscience lacking paper and a fountain pen. The inevitable slice needed for resurrection is bond to be purgatory: the misery of living off the same noose which we ourselves have finalized, as we scream: "I am tired! My heart is tired!" until we reborn into the core shape. My soul is cultivated more than ever. Its margins must be passed onto paper so I may live from what is left. That is the infinity of my existence. What subjects of heavens and dreary winters? Was I destined to be writing of travel with doors locked, windows closed? Was I destined to be writing of lovers with a maiden hand?

Everyone forgives me because I am doomed by nature and surroundings. I am a cozy, vulnerable caterpillar. I am a knife for meat, a despot. If I am not writing I am experiencing, if I am not

experiencing I am idling. Children of the apple tree
are impossible to love because we firmly believe
there is some good in them. Signing to be one you
have signed to loneliness. We flourish to abhor
florets we were devoted to therefore fate is lost.

Hanging on the edge, it becomes your home.
Margins are neither metal darkness nor alcohol of
love, they are just margins.

People have forgotten

Sun falling down, hiding cowardly under a salmon
blanket, knows nothing about dying nor life's last
determined layer. Life is a thunder very short and
it's wrong to live as if this was our last day, we
should live as if this was our only day.

Only days we lived were of a precious kind. As we
walked side by side forests changed their seasons
and wouldn't bear us any daisies, then we would sit
and reverie out loud, back then when your hair was
brown. Propaganda was fading away, you wouldn't
under any circumstances let the light in, pipes broke
and feces were on the street like in a ghetto. I did
my accounting, you did your translations, we shared
a cigar and cooked without a clue what to do.
I shouted at you for all that dust and mold, and you
promised me to gaze at stars from the attic some
night. I think we should have died by that gas leak,
with smiles of bright future and many dreams...

My dear daisy, nothing torments you now in her
embrace of white and gold sunrays shaped by
amiable air.

Reader, I do desire to reveal you wisdom of some
sort, retrieving, novel hope, novel prose, something
I was given by my unrequited foolishness. However,
all I've discovered is why Rimbaud never used his
second name, Nicolas, I suppose it sounds like
a name of some Ivy league sucker in a pink polo.
I close the right eye: greying, ancient May flowers,

I close the left eye: an ant who has trudged millions of voyages is overcoming manmade lines. My sleep is mere, yet deep. I keep waking up in dubious forecasts of hell with a tiny prickly pencil as I watch midnight geese nigh supermarket clean their feathers. Why would I cook without you if I can starve? My organs sing for you, love for you while they rot. And when I walk past her house she is always blasting music, living through her only days marked by your sugar opium lips.

Eternal Hills

to R. R.

I am the remnant of self. I am the remnant of a
tranquil being. Burn to the ground, your sireland
may not be your home. Like a tempest of widowers
you were gone. She had the same name as me,
you kissed under falling yellow leaves. Tears
dripped into my ears and I became deaf to my
surroundings out of ailment. I laugh about how
stupid everything was, that's all I do now.

Sulfuric acid, wildflowers shan't ever forget you.
This day you come to ponder forever, without
return, remembered as a wall of meat. Goodbye,
doom, outlying storm! I just want to tell you that I am
doing well, I am still writing. Perhaps I will read
some of my works to you when I'm dead.

Boxed wine

Why?

Why, deep dreamless sleep of alcohol hiding in shampoo bottles?

Deaf prunes still stood, shriveled under your return. You have been bestowing them the play of an old teaman in a young vessel until crude freezing wind smoldered along with his sisters snowflakes. Sister, what a word. Why could I not depart from heavens as her, in her right minds and pristine shield of virgin skin, and the fur of a pale lion, in a mask even more ancient than her missing heart?

Why? She has an upside-down cross between her legs, but why? If I weren't so lazy I could be a writer like that fisherman without a rod eating stewed fruit from a jar. Yet who do I beg for forgiveness, whose hair do I pull? Who do I stab, who do I endow with things I did not acquire easily? Snake nights twist in my babbling as I release Great Danes. The sister writhes on the ground of dry prunes.

Simone

Midmay nightingales, dear arrival, soon it might come and disappear in a ringful block. The plague of your fume crossed over centuries in a dignified raid on hearts... Flowers do sing. Curiosity is damned.

Vulgarly colorful leaves dissolved into rotting mud. Instead of love they collapsed into a pit digesting untouched sand. Yet again I come to reverie of nightly sky and this time it seems dead, no reply from the stars. Wicked blues fell upon the broken clock attached to my madness.

Slowburn

The grey is venting in black. It's a pity that nobody
acknowledges present while it's still present, only
after it becomes past.

Late night car rides, ceramic angel broke her wing.
Harrow, the fear of what shall be, its door has
a rusty handle and yellowish touch.

My body burns slowly. The last miserable scratches
of my heart haze about my own return.

Skinny Maria

My soul holds her in its arms instead of me.

What stays after the one who loses love?

Bones, just bones.

Maybe there is a teakettle floating in the universe and we don't know about it

I had whiskey to wash down the cake.

The land was muddy with the first leaves, yellow and scarlet stained greens. It blessed to branches in a dried state. As if remote planets, which names and sounds were useless and indifferent to the shallow kind, did not scan my suffering and trepidation at this hidden earthy place.

Love comes by foot and leaves by train. Not that it would flee. It mostly comes too late, other times you are the one who overslept. It also runs over many people. Insides like grenade blasts smudged along the railways, it's gruesome and fine, fine in some sort of perspective.

It was to be about longing for lost love and old books with dotted stains, words pressed backward on subsequent pages. You were made of love and mostly alcohol. I was made of rust only to let stars treat my sight. Do we fancy foolish angels, foolish masks? Materialism has a soul, a slush, it pisses with the door open. Maybe there is a teakettle floating in the universe and we don't know about it. Maybe somewhere else, beneath ardent overdone passage of trees you kissed me twice on cheeks and once on lips, and nevermore again.

A writer who cannot write leans onto a wet crumbled wall, I know it seems like I am not trying to get better at all. Past and future are abstract tenses, thoughts are the destruction ceasing its present pulp, must I heal, must I wake up. Perhaps forgiveness matters only to fictional orphans. They must be blonde, with faces like tasteless chewing gums. You can hear only their screaming, not mine. I cannot bring you back from a coma. Your legs bring you everywhere but you are still cursed, hindered, you need them and I know. Genius men seek out average women because they want to shine, it's gruesome but fine, fine in some sort of perspective.

Beans

We had to create a line to a furnace, kneel and tell it: "I am foolish, I am foolish, I am foolish." three times. Gone to remark Earth with an unbearable wound which might have echoed through time somewhere, it was a waste. Aspirations were forgotten.

Life, you hollow-eyed grandmother, what kind of beans did you put on my plate? I have decided to retract my intelligence. By the laws of nature, body is not to be free unless mind comprehends its division, existence, likewise besets rational stiffness. Its shell reaches the extent of merriness that is destined for every soul. Taking over and vanishing into the thoughts that distort the touchable seeking its core while the core is present above it.

It's quite a zany plea to be drunk. When I drink I turn into a real human.

And I just sob. My portion is way too big. The beans are still on the plate and I am already full. You have to eat it all, said the shadow crone. Oh, grandma, never do I feel that I've grown, why must I be strong for nothing? I am neither a soldier nor a lumberjack.

They teach us not to smoke and not to swear but nobody protects us from possible suffering of life. The gift of pain doesn't shine in daylight, it waits to hit the nail.

Nobody worries about the spooks of unknown infinity, the agony of failure awaiting behind the border of abstract "end" we see, but I do. The beans have made my head sick. And sick people need even more beans. Oh, the beans. The beans whistle by my window.

The leaves fall on the back of her grave

to Cecilia L.

The leaves fall on the back of her grave, bestowing
us the dazzling exuberance of cold restless winds.
Born old to depart young, it was a meeting well
fated.

Those fat fish, in a vile fishpond that our distant
uncle had bought in a hope of saving his business,
have never understood how there can be so much
rage in the world for nothing. No one, in fact, is able
to answer it, all we know is that we feed onto each
other like lice even when we pledge to not.

The consequences seldom might be worse than the
remembrance of trauma itself, as you age you
become more and more invisible to people.
Pervitine, debit card, hunger strike, sex within the
face of all, my dear lover lives, not so far, marked by
the leech between my legs.

Light forms stand nigh her humble underground
tomb. I could not say anything else than that I am
back on pills and my life is too interesting to believe
but too tedious to be a book. We await still with
a blank daydream boy of why. Why of the cease
not, however, why of the inevitable decay of their
existences' recollection.

Sweet, sweet melody, he shouts at people for
standing in his way. Who cannot love every day

cannot love at all: death has come alive and life
adead.

Never shall I be forgiven my deceit that
revealed my blackened heart

to E. S.

You dream with your eyes shut. Their subtle
pureness swam in the sky and you came to be the
salvation to my woebegone soul and to my filth of
the words not written.

By everything that happens I seem to be haunted
forever like slushed highway snow. Bristling paper
twists like maggots disabled to feast on the metal
claws of my terrible guilt. Metal never burns. It but
bends to lust and greed, and poems sometimes. For
I burnt your gentle skin, decapitated your feathers,
only then I have found my heart hollow. Everybody
has a groin stained with blood theirs or else's.

You dream with your eyes shut while they scream.
Yet, I am here, outside I still await, condemned from
my own self in a havenless purge.

Your flighty curls fall into every bottle I drink.

Purple heart, color of gods

to E. S.

Gone like a whisper of dust during summer wind.

Linen bees and pollen grass, they do trudge the snowy way together, they tracked us down by absinthe and celibacy.

I wish I could stick my head into the oven like Sylvia Plath. Purple is the color of gods and who lesser than god could drink the poison from its shell?

But why should I care? Why would I care for scripted purgatory which shall door the purple heart whilst you I have and have not?

Light of my days, soft fortune close like a ghost, tangled far from one another... It verily did appear that you were gone like a whisper of dust during summer wind.

You see, I am right here, on these pages, my soul is here, fresh as it is. At the time you will be reading me god will have already died or I will have already died. Oh lord, how he fears death, a lot. He takes maddened women to look at the nightly sky to make them cry.

Psychosis

The fence is low. Redfoliage anguish trembles in its
deterioration. Everything that determines me is my
current feelings.

You play for me, Sunday dress worn on Monday,
we live behind blinds like worms. When I peek
through them the clouds are showing me signs.

You keep leaving my corpse to rot on hoards of
paper while you dominate the moonlight. The cult of
body, beauty, it can only drink, it can only live. I still
remember you before the metamorphosis, if there
was any. The fence is low and I wonder whether to
jump over it. What I believe, how I feel, it is not how
it is. I don't know you nor myself. I just know that
good writing doesn't make a good person. Why
daisies, why charades of Satie and innocence?

The play of blue light, rhymes are telling me that
I stink. Longing for my disappearance, longing to be
sought... Love has aborted me hundred years ago.

Motels

Its lurching within my room, its tenuous sense when I touch it. Yet, would I know of light if I couldn't see it?

Temporary marks on walls, youth is fading away like a match and I never came to be someone's first love, not even once.

The arrival of light illusions is the arrival of hope. Is there hope, and more importantly, what is hope? I touched the stain of the sun with my fingertips. It was cold. If I couldn't see the sun I would not feel it. The expectations of my thinking are deceptions, artificial tomorrows built in my mind, so is despair and fear and all which glues. That golden eye is always in my head.

What do you want to do about it, tortured soul?

I want to cry.

I sat on a sidewalk and cried.

Swelling, wander

            to the seizer and lighter of my soul

I glimpsed into an eye of a dead carp out on a shore
and saw my fortune, underwater visions from
a peninsula were further and further, I voyaged
outlying to the sea as if I had a friend. Do you
possess a name, nameless spirit? Shall you return
home discerning the maps? Shall you return soon
by persecuting grips?

Indiscrete gardens, coffee too bitter, you kept
running away until you ran yourself over, turned into
weightless sand illuminating dangerous lands,
frozen sun and regular linen grass related to
another kind for eternity, hence I can think about it
hence it can be achieved. Barbarian vodka was
burning as our tongues whipped bonfires, asking
how stupid can a person be to wish for
a masterpiece.

Debris turned into ashes to be reborn on petals of
million orchids, that's what everybody lingers to
hear. Come to our forest and beach and opera
house, I'll find you. The haven of everyone, the
haven that cannot die living through condemnation
as we rip out your wooden planks and massacre
your boats because we would rather garnish them
for someone else, because we've grown out of your
spell. Somewhen in past, we were destined for each
other. You taught me to return before the rapture of
borderlessness drops itself to sleep. The haven of

forgotten seasoning with dead carps on the shore,
the living ones are unseen in their water, still on
their road within the heavenly kiss of a personal
hell.

Heretofore

Friendship is like a stone. I gave you the stone and you tossed it into a river. Its last words were: "Notion prevails. The form may overshadow the content but never the notion." Its ether capriced to the soft surprise of everyday beauty. Its soul is yet again filled with indeterminate love.

Heretofore I awed. Did ancient unsure tombs resolve the language? When? People become different as you swipe through the clock. I observe whatever shall be even though I mightn't comprehend all occurrences yet I would ponder about the callow blossom of cabbage until lone desks malformed into living insides, I would get called artist for that. Does nobody truly see, except for you and me, that when fine dust flies away from petals the flower is undressed? A poet is an inventor, the poet is a vagabond, lunatic, and king at the same time, the master of their words, and not everyone calling themself The poet is The poet?

I've always reckoned there cannot be a man more rotten than myself. All the letters are about me – I, I, I, you, I, sorrow, you and I, nature, I, scarcely nation or society. I have always appeared to coexist with struggle in any kind of society. I've felt dry and unlarge within great circles, pretentious among the common, the closest I have ever felt to home was next to asocials, addicts, mentally challenged, dreamers hiding behind gutters, and- Then you

interrupted me with words that every good author
writes about self.

Oh, unity, one is all and all is one although since the
second we are tangible we are firsted to decay.
What I really like about literature is that humans
change and their spirits die out without notice. True
art doesn't submit to manmade time, it is conserved,
the captured version of one world's realm.

Friend, my beloved, without you I seem to serve no
purpose. I finally reinvented tranquility.

Process

The poet has died. No more words were said. No more words were needed to be said.

You cannot make a sad life jolly but you can make it beautiful. Some people are destined to remain in torment but they have a choice to transform it into beauty or kindness seen by others. They can use art to nourish minds and hearts.

Simone, treasure your lover, treasure your peace. Never capitulate on something you used to be keen on because somebody has hurt your soul and you cannot see any more meaning to existence. It's a murder that will never be chastised.

No more words written.

Pretend to pray

The interest of all will forever be the deadliness and
magnificence of everything temporary. Cavity.
Paraffin steps, lovers, scratches and Judy. Still,
I am faithful to you, perhaps not with my body, yet
with my soul – profoundly. How to linger beneath
a blooded cross is how to hear the hay whisper, out
until the dark captures me. I suppose each person
has a different half of their heart from the one
whose half they are. Hence the world's end was
canceled: by change and better tomorrows. And the
bonfire you ceased above grew into a spark.